It all began this morning
  when my watch was beeping so.
I took a look at Clarence Clock —
  he thought it was eleven!

He said he wasn't feeling well —
he didn't want to chime.

And no matter how he tried he couldn't tell the time.

Later on, at ten o'clock,
I peeked in through the door.

Clarence looked unhappy,
  and his hands were showing four!

At noon I went inside for lunch and looked at him again.

Clarence still looked worried —
and his hands were showing ten!

That was when I made a call
and got the doctor 'round.